THE
SEVEN
LAWS
OF
SPIRITUAL
PURITY

Also by Two Workers

Becoming What You Are

THE
SEVEN LAWS
OF
SPIRITUAL PURITY

A GUIDE FOR THE NEW HUMANITY

TWO WORKERS

Radiant Books
New York

The Seven Laws of Spiritual Purity was originally published as *The Spirit of the Unborn* in 1918. Illustrations by Chris and Con Designs.

Illustrations © 2023 by Radiant Books

Library of Congress Control Number: 2023939499

Published in 2023 by Radiant Books
radiantbooks.co

ISBN 978-1-63994-036-3 (hardback)
ISBN 978-1-63994-037-0 (paperback)
ISBN 978-1-63994-038-7 (e-book)

*Dedicated to the Parents
of the Coming Humanity*

CONTENTS

Preamble

The Plea for Purity: The Seven Laws

Epilogue

PREAMBLE

I am the Spirit of the Unborn.
I come to plead for better bodies
in which I wish to live.

THE SPIRIT OF THE UNBORN

I AM THE SPIRIT OF THE UNBORN! I am the Spirit of *all* the unborn children of all the world. I am their sum total. Each one of them is a particle of Me.

I come to call upon the parents of today and of tomorrow with a plea for Purity.

But not alone to those do I direct My call.

For in younger people, too — who know not yet if they ever will be parents — there is impurity which, by its subtleness, hampers My true expression.

And not only to the living is My plea but to the dead. For in their future shall they live again on Earth, and in their earth life may become parents.

Hence: to *all* I speak. To all humanity, My Voice goes out.

Still your desires — and listen to My Voice!

THE COMING HUMANITY

I AM HERE TO BESEECH YOU to prepare for Me, the Spirit of the unborn children of the Coming Humanity.

I am the One and only One who represents them all. For I am He who is in the heart of *all*.

On behalf of the children of the New Humanity shall I speak in this book: especially for their sake is the Purity required for which I plead. Never shall one of them become the child of any parent who is not pure in every way.

You, who do not wish to purify yourselves — you may still beget children if you so desire, but you will have to be satisfied with whatever child may come to your home: to the impure parent, no pure and highly evolved child can ever again be born. Into the home of you who are impure and selfish can come only the ones who have not reached the stage where they can form a part of the New Humankind!

But not to you, O parents who are pure and unselfish, will anyone ever come who is not worthy of yourselves. Never shall you give birth to a child who is not all that can be expected of Future Humanity — all that is to be realized by it.

Only if the parents of the present generation purify their bodies and their habits, emotions, and thoughts can I, in My new bodies, express those qualities which will make the Earth a Heaven and life an eternal bliss.

I — the Spirit of the Unborn — have come to call together the parents of the New Humanity!

The time is nigh in which to divide the people of the world into those who are prepared to establish My New Humanity and into those who are not yet ready.

I come!

And listen, you who long for beauty in your children: once more, I call!

THE PLEA FOR PURITY

PURITY

THE SEVEN LAWS

One, still impure, shall not despair.
One, who is pure, shall not despise.
One, who but strives, stands closer
to the gateway which admits to
My New Humanity than ail who —
having seemingly attained —
still criticize and condemn.

1
PURITY FROM PASSION

OVER THE WORLD OF HUMANITY — over the cities and wherever people have made their homes — there hangs a cloud, a muddy, viscid, astral cloud of sensuality.

Looking out over the Earth from My pure spiritual realm, I see the globe enveloped in a red-brown-colored fog that emanates from humankind.

From hour to hour seems the foul mist to be growing thicker, its sickening stench ever more pernicious — caused by the continuity of sensual actions, sensual talk, and sensual thoughts of people.

Into that cloud, I must descend!

Through that almost impassable barrier, I, Spirit of the Unborn, must go — to find a new incarnation!

How — tarnished by its filthy stain before I reach the Earth — can you expect Me to find adequate bodies, fit for My pure expression, fit for the Coming Humanity?

~

Watchfully am I waiting for possibilities to incarnate in purer bodies, conceived by parents who live in purity, even when married.

Marriage — the sacred bond of love, to which I looked for an opportunity to find bodies created in purity — what have people made of it? It has been desecrated, degraded into an institution of legalized immorality, debased by the habitual seeking of carnal satisfaction.

This *must* be changed if you want Me to come! Only in *pure* bodies can I birth — I, the Spirit of the Future Humankind.

Creative power should be used by you for My sake: that I may find new bodies in which to manifest the best and highest that is in Me!

Creative energy is the godliest part of you; in it lies not alone your semblance with the Divine, but your own Divinity!

Therefore: *abuse it not!*

What have you done with it?

What are you doing with it?

Answer these questions in perfect honesty. I know the answer — without your telling Me; for from My World, I can observe the most hidden facts in yours.

~

That you may *think* and *know* and not rush thoughtlessly along in the customary rut; this is the purpose of My asking you:

Can I come to you and find in you the Purity which, for My full expression, I so urgently need? Or will the atmosphere around you, too, suffocate Me?

Am I too personal, too rigorous in the way in which I tear the bandages from a filthy sore on present humanity, even if not on *you*?

Stop listening to Me if you wish.

But then: never complain about the consequences of your indocility, of your persistence in willful ignorance. And know: *I see* — I see every act of yours, of past and present . . . and of future possibilities, too. And it is because I see a probability of your carefully considering these words — of your *living up* to them — that I find it worth My while to come and speak to you, just in the way I do.

~

I see! And what are the acts that I have to look upon?

Waste of creative energy, by old and young . . . even by the *very* young!

Whose fault is this? Who is to blame for the alarming spread of self-abuse and immorality among young children?

Your fault, O parents, who are not living My Purity! *Your* fault, O men and women, all you of mature age, who fill the atmosphere with emanations of your impurity. What you send forth in acts, emotions, and thoughts impacts others. And tender youth is extremely sensitive; by *it*, your influence is the most readily caught.

You are the ones to blame!

You, who have children — do you remember your motive for calling them forth? Was it with thoughts of love for those who might come to you? Or thoughtlessly, ruled by your passion, in sensory gratification?

And, within its sanctuary, as the body was being built — have you respected the sacredness of its development? Or is it true in your case, too: that many an illegitimate was conceived in greater love and in greater purity than the children of you who scorn?

⁓

Born of sin — of "the sin against the Holy Ghost," as it has been rightly called — most children grow up breathing in and absorbing the baneful influence of the (be it ever so hidden) sensuality in acts and thoughts of their surroundings.

Thus, sensuality is stimulated in them. Unwarned — for *who* will warn them? — lacking true knowledge about the most vital things, they can indulge in fatal, secret sins.

As a result: the weaklings, seeking what they call "pleasure," in prostitution of themselves and of others . . . All at the cost of Me!

For wherever they go, the cloud of sensuality always becomes darker and more impenetrable. Wherever they go, there is no place for Me! Their very exhalations would tend to smother Me.

And, sad to say: the greater part of today's humanity are *those people*!

Therefore, I call and call and call again for greater Purity.

But very few there are who seriously listen. And fewer still are willing to enlist in My army, which with intense determination will work for Purity — preparing the way for Me, the Spirit of the Unborn.

Patiently am I watching for rents in the stifling cloud — which anyone can make who strives for Purity.

Each one who tries can, to begin with, stop adding new material to the hideous, nauseous cloud. Each one who goes on striving can become like a little sun, a radiating center of luminous Purity, and pierce that ghastly cloud.

From My World, I cannot shatter it; for it is a hopeless task to cleanse and purify where humans continually sully.

But whenever anyone in your world tries, *I see* it and rejoice — and to them go My help. And with My help, their strength will grow, enabling them to make an opening through which I can come down to find unhampered expression — be it in their children or, if possible: *in themselves*!

~

I, the Spirit of the New Humanity, have come to plead with you: not only that in those who are yet to be born, you shall offer usable instruments for Me — but that *in you*, I, with My qualities, may find expression, so that you, too, may be worthy to of being chosen for the Coming Humankind!

I plead for Purity in every possible way.

In the first place: for purity of sex life — for a pure use of all creative powers, for creation only.

Stop wasting your most Divine energy in self-gratification of the lowest, coarsest kind! *Transmute* it, when not needed for the creation of new bodies, into the power of creating uplifting words and ennobling thoughts to help the world. Apply your generative powers to the regeneration of your own bodies. Then can I, the Spirit of the New Humanity, be born *within you*!

To men and women, and all young people, is My call, My plea for Purity!

Help Me, each one of you. Become a ray of spotless Purity around which the cloud of sensuality cannot exist.

~

Passion — the cause sown in the past, resulting now in painful childbirth, endless physical and mental disorders — is going on to cause still worse afflictions till it is conquered. Passion is the abnormally stimulated Divine impulse — grown beyond control by vicious habit, by continued undue thought. You are its slave — because you have given it power over you.

Do not place the blame on your Creator for it all! You have developed this natural force into an artificial abnormality. Now, you will have to conquer it. This, you — each one of you — *must* do before you will be ready to receive Me.

Where you wish Me to come and build a body, even the sowing of the seed should take place without passion. Just as the pleasure of intoxicants and of strongly seasoned food is apt to naturally vanish when a person purifies their ways of living and of thinking — so will the passionate satisfaction of sexual intercourse entirely fall away from those who travel on the road toward perfect Purity.

The Coming Humanity, rising above the domination of the senses, will know no passion; it will have acquired — and live — that purer, greater love that seeks no bodily gratification. Only for love's sake, for the love of the yet unborn, will the New

People fulfill Nature's most holy function — giving to the to-be-incarnated souls the highest it *can* give.

Free yourself from passion!

Thus, will you help yourself, as well as help Me. For with every step you take toward greater Purity, a greater joy — abundant, pure, and *lasting* joy — awaits you.

2
PURITY FROM CRIME

Freedom from crime I want, wherever I come down!

Not alone from what you in the present time think of as crime — but from what I, the Spirit of the New Humanity, consider to be such.

Acts now called criminal are the coarsest instances of what *is* criminal in My terminology.

Millions of people now will disagree with Me. But all will share My viewpoint . . . when they are ready to become members of the Future Humankind — when they have climbed to where they can manifest Me.

As long as you are of a different opinion, you are not quite ready for Me!

As long as you go on killing or have creatures killed *for* you — you cannot be accepted in My soon-coming Humankind.

I need bodies unstained by bloodshed, unblemished in every way. Nor may there be a trace of cruelty in the hearts where I shall be born!

⁓

No slaughtering shall there be where I go! For slaughtering, even for food, is a breaking of My Law — the Law of Love.

You, who think it necessary because you *do not* think; you, who do not like to think about it because you *like* it so much; you, who fills your stomach with corpses for fear of becoming one — know this: that the soul of every creature which is killed by, or for you, sets up an obstacle on the road between you and Me!

No matter what you are devouring: be it meat or fish or fowl — I consider you a criminal, your food impure and foul.

Think!

Think about how you value life's manifestation in *yourself*. So does each thing that lives! Think of the wondrous structure which Nature has built up even in the smallest creature which you — unnecessarily, as many can prove — are chewing as food.

Think! Think yourself now into its consciousness. Look through its eyes — those beautiful, pure eyes through which Life (which *is* God) looks out into the world.

Feel the death blow that strikes it — if it is not tortured by pitiless proceedings, such as being slowly bled to death or boiled or skinned alive so that *your* palate may be tickled by more "delicious" food! Then feel its fear and hatred of humanity — which go out into the atmosphere and must impact human beings in the form of suffering.

Much of *your* suffering — against which you are rebellious and which you call unjust — may be the consequence of your own slaughtering in the near or distant past.

Know: there is no injustice in the Universe! What comes to you, *you* have caused; what you now do to others, by deed or word or thought, will impact you at some time.

You say *you* never kill — but have it done *for* you? Then, twofold is your crime! First, you are guilty of the death you cause, and — thoughtlessly, I suppose — you encourage cruelty in some of your fellow beings, impelling them to deeds for which they, in their future, have to suffer. Both will impact *you*!

I know your reasoning: *something* must be destroyed to keep your body fed. But it is within your power to bring destruction down to the less evolved things — to cause *less*, ever less suffering. Even the killing of the vegetable kingdom can be avoided, if you will it so: when your compassion grows and takes that in. For on the fruit of assiduous plants, human beings can exist.

It is for you to expand your love, so you can live without slaughtering.

No — you need not fear that cattle and game will be so plentiful (when not killed off by you) that they will overrun your gardens and your cities and your homes. Nor will they take your food.

Love, as the basis of your attitude and actions, will never bring ill to you. Love is the basis of Creation, the fundamental Law of the whole Universe. Where love is lived, this Law itself is set in motion to adjust conditions and harmonize all things.

~

Vivisection? I shudder when I think of it!

How is it possible that people could be so mis-led by mental fallacies they commit — even indulge in — this scientific crime?

Humanity — in your hands was placed the care of the defenseless, dumb creatures to lead them, lift them up to a more highly evolved stage. They are your *younger siblings* — all of one family in the Creator's mind.

You stand accused of a crime!

For you have not alone enslaved, ill-treated, and exploited the helpless ones for selfish purposes — but starved, and frozen alive, sliced, ripped and sawed, burned, baked and butchered, scalded and scalped God's living creatures. Unscrupulously dabbling in the blood and agony of sentient, sensitive beings, you have caused excruciating pain by the cowardly and cursed practice of vivisection.

Instead of older siblings and loving guides, you have been vicious brutes and monstrous torturers.

This still goes on!

Pity the poor "little ones" who, by the thousands, serve the experiments.

But, after all, have more pity on those deluded beings who *do* the experiments! For the effects of their willful cruelty will be terrible. No one can keep from them what — after death and in other lives on Earth — they shall experience. All acts react — such is the Law. By their own frightfulness, they have stored up a great cause for suffering. This *must* work out on them — that they, by suffering, may learn to spare and protect all things that live.

Have pity on *them*!

But do not dodge your responsibility. You have helped — *are* helping *yet*, I fear — to strengthen and encourage the vivisector in committing inhuman deeds.

By your own cruelty — be it of ages past — you have created, in super-ethereal matter, thought entities, which, gathered together, intensify the experimenter's horrible inclinations. Then, by your approbation, or by protesting only half-heartedly, or by indifference on this vital point, you are *partakers* of the crime.

Do you approve of vivisection because you think (erroneously though it be) that it helps to cure disease? Remember then: pain and disease result from a breaking of the Law and cannot be overcome by breaking the Law *again*. The cosmic Law of Love and Justice cannot be evaded.

Perhaps you still believe that vivisection may help to prolong your life or that of those near and dear to you. But even if this *were* true and possible: I would rather have no bodies than ones kept alive at the cost of the suffering of whatever creature it be!

This viewpoint must be *yours* if you wish to side with Me!

～

Your laws forbid murder — and yet you murder murderers *by law*! Only distorted brains can deem this logical! But human laws and brains lack perfection, and both still lack Purity.

When I am born in the children of the Future Humanity, there will be purer brains and *no* laws but *the* Law — i.e., the Law of Love.

They will live by this Law and need no *human-made* laws. And they will know more than you now *can* know.

But even you should know: in a criminal, the *body's owner* is diseased; the entity *within* is the one who commits the crime, using the body as its instrument.

You may kill the body — but the entity itself *lives on.*

You liberate the entity — who, after the execution, is much more dangerous than before. For — filled with revenge and hatred, in addition to other wrongs — it will go on spreading, unchecked in any way, its ominous influence.

Caught in the body, you can limit the depraved actions of the indwelling entity, control it, and *better* it. Thrown out of its physical vesture, beyond human control, it gravitates toward those with similar vicious propensities — inciting them to villainous acts, using them as its tools, its mediums for revenge.

Thus, legalized murder makes *more* murderers.

Therefore, again: kill not — not even criminals. Their death does not help you — nor does it help them.

Restrain their actions while you cure their souls. Treat them as patients, for they are morally sick.

Their souls are young — young as your own once was — and weak and ignorant. Give them your own wisdom, your own moral strength. Apply the Law of Love!

If you really *are* the older, more highly evolved one, your duty is to help, to guide, to teach, to *love*. But if you continue to execute and despise, you are not yet far evolved above the criminal. You are then guilty of a lack of understanding and love — which results in all crime.

~

No hunting can there be — be it for fashion's sake or as a sport — where I shall manifest. Whoever does it, or causes it to be done, commits a serious crime against My moral code, which is wholly based on love.

Your furs which you are so fond of because they cost so much (their price was the suffering and the life of animals, which, indeed, is far *too* much!); your feathers, torn from slain (oft only injured birds, whose nests of young are left to starve — that *you* may go about with a "fashionable" hat; the skin of unborn bodies, cut from the mother's womb to give *your* hands a *soft* covering.

Seeing all this hurts every cell in Me, and where such things are worn, I must stay afar.

Do you not realize that such ornaments are laden with a *curse* — and that each one who touches them for greed's or vanity's sake will be subjected to its fatal influences?

Do you not realize that your adornment is detestably distasteful in the eyes of anyone who — as I — can see and sense the pain and anguish attached to it?

You, many of you — on the ground of moral principles, of tenderheartedness — would never think of doing with your own hands what you allow others to do *for* you.

But you are just as guilty — if only of a lack of love, which counts heavily with Me — as the one who kills for your ill-chosen means of comfort and satisfaction.

~

Killing for sport, for amusement, is an atrocious thing — incomprehensible to all the children of the Humankind that is to come.

Did you ever saunter through a field or forest on a lovely day when the deep blue of the sky, the golden sunshine on the trees and foliage, and the fresh green grass and shrubs work as an inspiration? Could they "inspire" you then to go and *kill* something?

Did you ever come across the bloody trail of a wounded animal or find a dying creature, shot but not killed outright by hunters, wantonly "sporting"? Or did you see an animal caught in the iron jaws of a cruelly squeezing trap, and see its agony, its desperate efforts to regain its liberty?

Could you then go and kill — kill these life-loving creatures who, like yourself, enjoy the happiness of existence in the realms of bounteous Nature? Could you still go, destroying these unsuspecting, living things — just for the sake of boasting about the numbers *you* had killed?

Then go and do those things if you cannot resist the longings which make you thirst for murder and for blood. But do not think that where I am, *you* ever can come near. The joy and beauty of the New Humanity will be protected from your influence — for your mere presence would defile its Purity.

Even hunting beasts of prey will not be done by those who aspire to form a link with Me.

Such creatures are the outcome of your own cruelty. As, in the past — in lives long past — you trained domestic animals to help you on your hunts, *you* have evolved those species you now fear. You have imbued them with *your* cruelty. Beast preys on beast because *people* taught it so. All murderous instinct — in all creatures — is of human origin!

Great is the guilt of humans toward the animal kingdom. When will humanity be willing to expunge its debts and — by deeds of mercy and kindness — obliterate its outrageous transgressions?

Humanity was, and *is*, the one discordant note in Nature's symphony — the one blot on the work of the Creator. Humanity has become a menace to the consummate fulfillment of God's plan. Yet meant to be — and still *destined* to be — its most glorious culmination.

Humanity was given self-consciousness, the power of thought, to unfold its Divine qualities. Greatly abused have they the godlike gift that was bestowed upon them.

But in the future, they will attain self-consciousness — and know all Life as One. Then will they undo the evil that in the past they did. Then they will learn to love *all* as they love themselves now.

~

Yes — even vermin, even what you call "pests"!

They are the outcome of your hatred of evil human thoughts. Think not that just by "killing," you can free yourself from them. Your own thoughts live in them. And those will take new forms — with venom intensified, caused by the horrid feelings with which you still can kill.

These are the facts known to the ones who fully know the Law — facts visible in subtler realms, invisible to humankind, blinded by self-made obstacles of ignorance and sin.

Study — and *live* — the Law. Then you will know and see!

Your envy and your ill-temper; your greed and mercilessness; your stinging criticism; your own uncleanliness; your secret, ugly thoughts which you have been sending out so superabundantly from day to day and almost every hour — all these instill into vermin the very qualities that make them a nuisance to you.

Destruction of the forms will *not* destroy the thoughts essential to the vermin's life. But you must stop your hatred, your fear, your unkind thoughts. Only by purer thoughts — only by thoughts of love — can you eradicate the power which, in the past (be it only yesterday), you have stirred up by your own loveless thinking.

Sages — and even ordinary human beings — have *proven* that no beasts or vermin bother those who live the Law of Love . . . that is: who love all Life.

Someday, you will know as I know: that the One Life is manifested in *all*. To kill is to rob Life of its form — which, after all, is robbing God of a form for His expression.

All Life is He.

Life, the mysterious power humankind can never control, is the Divine Itself — the One Reality in all, in you, in Me.

3
PURITY FROM POISON

WHY DO YOU ALL — or almost all — eat poisons, drink them, breathe them, and inject them into your blood?

Just because others do it? Through thoughtless habit? To please your physical senses? For fear of sickness and of death? To seek forgetfulness from troubles and from boredom? Or, for what other reason?

None of these motives appear very sound to Me. None of these could influence the spiritually evolved, who seek the Purity that the New People will have.

To those People, not only will the present use of poisons seem the greatest folly — but the arguments for their use will be quoted as proof sufficient of the lamentable state of moral and mental development of today's humanity.

The lack of individual convictions; the giddy-headedness; the willing submission to the rulership of bodily wants and don't wants; the ignorance about the continuity of conscious existence; the weakness of attempting to elude life's lessons — all these are proofs of a young stage of evolution, which has to be outgrown before admission into the Coming Humankind can be obtained.

No poison will impair the Purity of that enlightened generation!

Meat — is it necessary for Me to tell you that it is poisonous, in addition to the fact that crime is attached to it?

Not only are the animals frequently diseased; not only do you make a graveyard of your own digestive organs, and thus pollute your body with the decaying remnants of cadavers; but also is their blood the carrier of animal qualities; by eating meat, you build those into you. You strengthen animalism in yourself, which you are intended to outgrow. And the anger, fear, and hatred which fill the animals as they are slaughtered — these go into their blood . . . and poison *you*.

It makes you irritable, emotional, and restless; it stirs up your passions, setting up a thirst for fiery drinks and spices.

All kinds of reasons there are — hygienic, physiological, economical, ethical, occult — why you should not eat meat. Read, if you like, the "pros" of swallowing it — and also read the "cons." Then (without worrying about the shape of your teeth or the length of your intestines) look around and see the convincing fact: many live quite joyously *without* it.

But above all this, bethink what I now say: no blood may pass the lips of those in whom I shall manifest! And not a single creature shall be allowed to die or suffer for their sake.

~

Alcohol . . . yes, taken in quantity, you all agree that it is detrimental. But you should also know that *every drop* of it is poisonous.

Whether gulped down the throat as liquor, carefully apportioned as a medicine, sniffed up in perfume, rubbed into the skin, natural or camouflaged, or when denatured — it is always injurious to moral and mental as well as to physical health. And every bit of it — its faintest odor in the atmosphere — draws undesirable entities who make the world around you impure. In this way, too, it is poison for you and those close to you.

It may briskly stimulate, inciting wit, quick action, and a sensation — though deceptive — of feeling extremely well. It acts like a flaring fire: a brilliant display followed by desolation.

In reality, it *dulls*. Dulls brain capacity. Dulls the keen sensitivity of the nerves. Dulls the ability to judge sensibly. Dulls the digestive powers. Dulls muscular vigor. Dulls moral stamina. Dulls clear vision. Dulls practically every organ.

Most harmful of all: it dulls — even when taken in minutest quantities — those organs which, in latent potentiality, contain humanity's power of superphysical vision; and, more than that: of *spirituality*. Long discarded and unused — put and kept out of operation by humanity's own impurity — these organs will be revived in the children of My People.

Only by Purity — not alone from alcohol, but from all passion and poison — can they regain their true function.

~

What has been said of alcohol applies to opium, morphine, and other drugs. And even tobacco. For nicotine *is* poison — albeit that some can smoke and live a hundred years.

Tobacco soothes — which is to say: it stupefies emotions, nerves, mind, and all those faculties which are also affected by the use of alcohol.

Although not criminal like eating meat, not tending toward crime like using alcohol — smoking, in one way, is more apparently objectionable than either. The smoker, with their pernicious habit, pollutes the atmosphere to the disgust and danger to the health of those around them. First, with their smoke, and afterward, with their breath and nauseous, evilly magnetic emanations, they make themselves an offensive nuisance.

The disregard for the interests of others, by which the smoker proves their utter selfishness — this in itself would make it quite impossible for any member of My Future Humankind to smoke.

~

The most dangerous group of poisons — though scientifically prescribed — are vaccines, serums, and all those obnoxious things which you allow to be injected, infecting your very blood. This superstitious practice, this dangerous medical craze, is the most ludicrous fallacy of science run amuck.

Wild tribes looked most reverently at the dances and performances of their "wise" sorcerers (how foolish!).

Your ancestors submitted most trustfully to the crude bloodletting operations by their "wise" medics — who eagerly applied it to whatever ailed the crowd (how stupid!).

You now (how, what?) most confidingly permit your medical faculty to let putrid, septic matter contaminate your blood.

Worst of all, these serums — themselves products of disease — have been obtained at the cost of suffering: by vivisectional experiments on animals and occasionally on humans!

For this, more than any other reason, the practice of inoculation stands *condemned* in the New Humanity!

There, disease will be prevented. Not by absorbing poison or by injecting pus — but by sane and sanitary living, by the purity of food, of every deed, of thought.

Only by Purity!

～

It is habits — senseless habits — that you are addicted to. They poison your existence and spoil your pure joy of life.

By your habits — thoughtless habits — you have built up the instincts and the cravings of your body, which demand obedience of you. You have become slaves of habit instead of masters of destiny!

By habit, you do all you do. By habit, you slur through life — grasping all passing pleasures . . . instead of winning that great and permanent joy that comes with Purity and freedom from the rulership of habits.

My People will have entirely risen above the poisonous dominion of restricting growth-impeding habits!

4
PURITY FROM PETTINESS

You, Gods-to-be — you, who would know that you *are* God if you but knew your Self, what are you yet but tiny tin-gods on a homemade pedestal? Hollow at that, both base and statuette; inside them, naught but choking air with which you inflate your self.

It would be amusing . . . if it were not so pitifully petty, if pettiness were not the keynote of your lives! Please note: it is not your neighbors that I have reference to — but decidedly to the pettiness *in you*.

Review your days.

Consider the motives for each deed carefully. Weigh on a balance all your selfishness: all that you did to please and glorify your own personality. And on precision scales, measure your love: all you did for others, in perfect selflessness. (I hope you will find a pair sufficiently sensitive.)

Compare the two results.

Then say whether you would still blame Me if I stated that your whole life seems petty.

~

How, in the mornings, do you get up?

Just sluggishly because your shop, office, and routine work need attention? Or sometimes gleefully, when you look forward to an agreeable happening: a trip, a party, a present, some special profit, or the visit of someone that will give *you* joy?

Did you ever greet the daybreak buoyantly, filled with the thought of what this day may enable you to do *for others' sake*? To lessen pain, to impart happiness, to help with all the means that you have at your disposal — not alone by what you have, but by all that you can be?

This is how all My Children will arise: filled with that purest joy of self-forgetfulness. If yours are other motives, they are petty.

⁓

What do you work for?

Just for the daily bread of your own family? To add to your material possessions? To keep up — or improve — your social standing? To acquire a name for yourself and maybe fame?

Or, for the betterment of conditions for your fellow people — even if no salary, no write-ups in the papers, no recognition from any side, results from it for you?

Is petty selfishness, or unreserved selflessness, your incentive?

⁓

What did you have a family for? What did you marry for?

Just because *you* wanted happiness? Because you thought of the pleasure and the comfort that it would bring to you? Even with so-called love: did you not mostly consider the advantages that it would have for you? Do not pretend that you did it for love's sake, if in reality, it was for self's sake, to accommodate the puny, selfish "you"!

My Children will not be led by any such petty thoughts. Only unselfish reasons will guide their every step. As a result, they will experience a happiness you — with the utmost brain strain — have no idea of.

~

What are you eating for — three, four, five times a day?

Do you eat to live and to be able to work better — or do you work, and apparently only live, to eat better, in a more epicurious way?

Are dinners and delicacies still desirable attentions to be offered to your friends — by them again to be repaid to you?

Do recipes for new dishes, soups, pies, and desserts still fill a large percentage of your daily talk and thought?

Is your kitchen still your shrine room, the cooking stove, the altar on which you bring offerings — blood offerings at that — to the highest you can worship?

Is your stomach still the sun of your existence, around which a system of numerous "plan-eats" and "come-eats," in dyspeptic disharmony, everlastingly revolves?

Then, pettiness (I am sorry) is paramount in you.

~

Why do you dress — in full or in half dress?

To protect your body from weather influences — which can be done in graceful simplicity?

Or: to parade; to make others think that you are somebody; to proudly revel in the beauty others cannot have; to be admired; to excite jealousy; and to attract attention?

If so — go on, you slaves of fickleness and fashion. Do not let Me bother you. Continue being petty; indulge in hats and haberdashery and expensive petticoats. On *you*, I need not count for the establishing of the glorious, free New Humanity!

~

Why have you a religion or a philosophy? Why do you go to church or to religious meetings?

Because your parents do? Because it is customary? Because it gives a splendid opportunity to make acquaintances? To ensure a reserved seat in Heaven? Because a ceremony, or a well-worded lecture, makes you feel — through emotionalism — exceptionally good? Because your concrete mind delights in definitions and speculations about vague and far-off things?

None of these petty reasons seem plausible to Me. Only as an expression of your inner Divinity, as an irresistible desire to realize your inherent link with God — thus only are religion or philosophy true values, instead of spurious shams.

~

Your very virtues are, too frequently, petty vices in disguise. Some of you are so full of virtue that you make yourselves unbearable and, by your self-complacency, cause pain to others. True virtue never harms.

You are very kind — *sometimes*, when conditions are suitable, when you are in the right mood, when it may serve your special purposes. If you are truly kind, you are *always* kind and make no distinctions.

You are charitable — on official subscription lists.

You give liberally — in order to gain, no matter what: love, friendship, recognition, satisfaction, and gratitude.

You are full of joy — when everything goes well with you.

You are humorous — no matter whether it may hurt somebody's feelings if people call you smart. Your humor only humors your vain personality.

You love to do your work perfectly — in order to excel and be considered more than others.

You adore the beautiful, in music, in all art — with the one wish: to have it for your own enjoyment and glorification. What your rival has, or has produced, cannot be beautiful, of course.

You long for spiritual development — not that you may help others, but to *be helped*, in order to become more than your fellow people — not to serve the world, but to *rule* and gain authority.

I know your motives — better than you do yourself. I shall not undervalue a single one of you. But you must know yourself: your little "self" first, with all its pettiness — before you can know your Self.

~

Why do you talk — *and* talk?

About the weather; about your health; about your food; about your own affairs, and even about those of others; about people whom you know — but usually do *not* know; and about all kinds of petty nothingness?

Is it just a habit which you cannot stop?

Can you not grow beyond the stage of prattling children? It is worse than that: a child's talk is innocent — is *yours* always? When you gossip? When you repeat an unkind story about friends or strangers? Do you know their motives, all their difficulties, the lessons they have to learn, the struggles they have to fight? If you did, you would not speak about them like you do.

Is there nothing better to be done than to indulge in this petty talk, *talk*, talk? You waste your time and energy — your opportunity to hear the wise and loving Voice of your true Self.

You do not even know that there *is* such a Voice? Because you talk too much! Because you are always occupied with your petty little "self" and its material interests!

My children in the Coming Humanity will know and understand the Voice of Self — and readily listen to it.

And then do not forget that sound *creates*. Speech is a creative force. The manifested Universe was actually created by the Divine Word. So, too, do *your* words create.

Every word you utter, every noise you make, sets up a vibration in the physical ether. Where does it stop — and when? Nowhere — and never! It goes out and out — and on and on. Your chattering and jabbering disturb the harmony of the whole Universe! And for eternity, the origin of the disturbance can be traced back to *you*.

Better be silent than abuse this mighty creative force in senseless, thoughtless, useless, aimless, endless talk!

⌇

Why do you live — and die?

Do you think there is no reason for such events as birth and death? Do you think they are just "happenings"? Or do you not think at all?

Do you only live because you cannot help it and die without knowing why? Do you *fear* death, for fear of losing "life," losing all your property, losing consciousness of "Self"?

The time will come when you will realize that your own life is *eternal*. Then will the "self" — that petty, selfish "self" with all its separateness — appear to you like an unwieldy load hindering your growth.

Better shake that burden off while you are what you call "living,": for death will not free you from it.

Un-self yourself. Then will you really — and forever, in unbroken consciousness — live!

Perhaps you think that — though there may be a reason for life as well as death — you are not supposed, not even *allowed* to know?

You — created in the likeness of the Almighty God — do you think you can be like Him without omniscience? You *are* He — in latency, in undeveloped powers. But by your pettiness, you limit His expression!

Investigate! Think! Know! Unfold your latent powers! *Become* almighty — and omniscient! No expression of life is too insignificant — nothing too great for your understanding. There is no secret in the Universe that you are not to know!

Outgrow your pettiness!

Throw off the chains which limit your self-expression: your trifling habits and imaginary duties, your thoughtless going-on along customary ways, your fear of differing from your surroundings, your fear of *anything*.

All that belongs to the "self" must go. Then — and then only — manifests the Self.

Set to work — and do not despair.

Even the biggest fool will evolve into a tool in the hands of the Great Architect, who will finally express the glory of His Being through all His creatures.

Hasten the process of your evolution.

Thus, will you speed the coming of My lofty, fearless Humanity!

5

PURITY OF SOCIAL CONDITIONS

UNSOLVED SOCIAL PROBLEMS throw a black shadow upon present humanity: problems of capital and labor, of wealth and poverty; of child's welfare, and of destitution of invalids and aged; of wages and working hours, of overwork and unemployment; of vice and unutilized benevolence; of crime and charity; of hygiene and disease; of tenements and untilled land; of power for the few, and slavery for the many; of trusts and lack of trust; of money and lack of money!

These problems are the weeds in what could be the enchanting, luxuriant garden of human civilization. But you have mistaken them for permanent growth. You have protected *them* instead of the superb vegetation that you were intended to foster — until they have smothered all the more delicate plants, which need full sunlight and need to be bathed in rays of Divinity.

The weeds were easier to grow. Now they have grown above your heads — thick as a forest — and you begin to feel the chill that hangs in their shadow. You long for sunshine — and try to trim and clip the gigantic weeds in order that a little ray may penetrate you.

Do you contemplate cutting the plants to get *more* warmth, *more* light? Be careful what you do! If the root remains, it will sprout again: your cutting will not help until you pull out the root. That root is selfishness! Not alone in others — but in *you*!

Clean out that little plot that has been entrusted to you! To clean those of all your neighbors is far too great a task: that is not expected of you. First, clear your own — and do it for *their* sake: that they may be able to enjoy the light thrown on your garden and the beauty of the tender plants of Love, with fragrant blooms of Purity that will take the place of weeds.

Then — seeing what you have done and attained — they will soon follow your example and readily accept your unobtrusive help. Before long, no weed will remain. Its roots will be destroyed. And no more shadows will be cast by the outcome of selfishness upon the joy of being part of the community.

Then will My People spread out over the Earth, abiding in those Gardens of selfless Love and perfect Purity, which you can now prepare. And you — by the power of your un-selfed Self — will belong to that sublime New Humankind and, with the others, will enjoy the fruits of the prolific plants you must now guard and cherish.

⁓

I do not deal with each problem separately. I shall not show you how to potter about repairing leaks, replastering here and there, and covering with fresh paint soiled spots on your tottering building of civilization.

Keep it up as best you can. Go on living in it . . . until a new home shall be ready.

In the meantime: combine your efforts with erecting a New Building. Lay the foundation of all-enduring selflessness, raise the walls of protective love, and decorate with irreproachable purity. Provide, for all alike, the furnishings of universal thoughts and joy.

Then move — and leave behind your trash of social problems: you will have neither place nor use for them.

Keep the old structure as a museum with relics of a queer and foolish past. No one will ever want or need to live in it again, provided: you do your share in helping to construct the new edifice — provided you join the workers preparing the world for the beauteous New Humanity.

~

Problems exist only for the ones who are still ignorant. To those who guide human evolution — to the Teachers of the child humanity — your social problems no longer exist. Once having solved them for Themselves, They know.

Why, then, do They not come and help you solve them? Would it help a child in school if the teacher solved its simple little arithmetic problems? It would be easy for the teacher — but would it train the child? Would, in that way, the child develop the qualities and the capacities for the purpose of which the problems are laid before it?

Wise teachers watch the children lovingly, rejoicing when a pupil, by their own exertion, has solved a problem. Then, they advance that pupil and give them harder problems — until the school years are over and the children graduate.

Thus do they, the Teachers of present humanity, consider social problems. They have laid them before you — that you, in solving them, may develop your inherent powers! *You* must work them out without the Teacher's help.

~

In the meantime, I am waiting for you to graduate. Graduating from this generation means admission into Mine: into that illumined Humankind into which all can be born.

But I cannot wait indefinitely! I cannot wait for all those who are lazy, who would rather play than work at the problems, who try to evade the training, and who seem to believe that the purpose of the tasks is to make life miserable!

Only those who apply themselves cheerfully, glad of the training which will enable them to do *better* work later — those only can be candidates for My Coming Humanity.

I have come to help them — to hasten their promotion. A hint is all that I can give. But it contains the key to the solution to all difficulties.

Listen, you who seriously struggle with your problems, anxious to solve them: Love is the key that will open the secret chamber — the chamber of the human heart — where you will find the ever-present solution which will make all problems vanish from your existence.

Take that key.

But remember: it works only if it is handled with immaculate Purity!

~

Until you have discovered that Love is the only key to solving your problems, your lessons have not been learned: you cannot graduate.

As you refuse, life after life, to learn — you are handed over to a private Teacher who never fails. Strong, patient, forgiving, compassionate, filled with the one desire to help you to grow toward greater happiness, toward the Future Humankind — and with perfect knowledge of your failings and your possibilities, this Teacher takes you in hand. You may not like the method — but it is the greatest help that could be given to you.

The name is Suffering.

No greater — and more loving — Teacher ever was than Suffering!

Unfailing is the ultimate result. When nothing else brings out love and compassion — your own suffering *does*. It makes you understand what others feel; it makes you feel *with* others, thus sowing the seed of Love.

Not always does this grow immediately.

It may have to drill its way through a crust of stony ground before its tiny shoot becomes visible on the surface. And Suffering may have to help, to break the ground and loosen it, and keep it soft.

This Teacher — the liberator of the Divine in humankind — continues to bear with you, with your obstinately clinging to selfish interests . . . until you have learned the lesson: unburdened yourself from "self," and begun to live in the Self.

Pain is the shortcut toward liberation — toward a conscious realization of Life and Light Divine. It is the dark tunnel through which all must pass to reach the land of unfading beauty, eternal youth, and bliss.

As you advance into the tunnel, the darkness deepens, with no beam of light behind, no glimmering ahead; the air is heavy; you awkwardly grope about to find your way; you fear a cave-in; you are near exhaustion and bitterly complain.

Go on, go on! Listen to the sounds ahead. They are the cries of ecstasy of those approaching the opening at the end who begin to see what you cannot yet see: the colors and the splendor of light such as they have never seen, which will be yours forever once you arrive there.

Listen again: footsteps coming toward you, glad voices calling you. It is they who have had a glimpse and now come back to encourage you, to cheer you, to share their joy with you. For they have seen the light of the new era — which only instills joy when it is shared with others, with all who can be reached.

⌒

There *is* another way to the valley of blithe felicity. It is a long and weary way, zigzagging across high mountaintops through fields of never-melting snow. It is a lonely road full of dangers: where avalanches threaten, where one easily loses their path, freezing to death in solitude.

Some try that road, but they either become lost or, eventually, return — to pass into the tunnel.

No human creature ever reached their goal, except through the Tunnel of Suffering!

~

All is well!

All that is *is* well as it is and for the good of everyone concerned. But that is not excluding the fact: it might — and *will* — be better.

Are you not yet convinced that in a universe ruled by Love — of which the Almighty Ruler *is* Love itself — there can be no injustice?

Even the greatest suffering, as well as the slightest unpleasant experience, is self-attracted. Not as a punishment, laid upon you by the wrath of an avenging Power, but as the natural reaction of your own actions, of your own stubborn refusal to learn life's lessons, your continued seeking to serve the "self," instead, and at the cost, of Self.

Perhaps you are conclusively aware of this fundamental truth: that *nothing* is unjust and that to every creature is meted out only a well-deserved share of evil as well as good. You may have this wisdom at hand and freely make use of it whenever others are in trouble, in sorrow, in serious difficulties. But — when some disappointment thrusts itself upon *you*, where is your wisdom then? You are provoked and angry, worried, unnerved, upset — and call whatever strikes you: unwarranted, undeserved, unjust!

You are blinded by the "self." Wake up; take your own medicine with the impersonal wisdom of the Self.

Suffering — and every blow that you ascribe to fate — is a medicine of your own making. You brewed it by your past deeds; it is *yours* — every drop of it. But by the Ones Who guide your evolution, it is lovingly applied to cure you . . . from yourself!

Hence: all is well.

Even the misery of your present social conditions . . . as long as they remain as they are.

But: things will not be as well with you as you wish them to be, as long as you have not exhausted every means whereby to alleviate your kin's suffering — from whatever cause that be! Things *cannot* be what you call "well" as long as you still need to repeat the same lessons — until you have learned goodwill and compassion.

⁓

Outer conditions are the outcome — the mirrored picture — of inner qualities. This counts for individuals as well as for a generation.

You, in your world of unrealities, try to remodel the ephemeral reflections — your social conditions — by some sketching and painting on the surface of the mirror. Do you not see the *originals* — your inner qualities — as the things that should be changed to improve their own reflection?

The change for the better can only come from within — from within *yourself.* First, purify yourself — then will conditions change.

This is not a selfish way — nor a self-centered one. To succeed, you must rid yourself of "self"; and void of "self" — how *could* there be a question of selfishness?

As you purify yourself, you grow from "self" to Self — toward unity with all. And then you cannot help loving and helping all. Further: your own perfection helps to perfect the whole of humanity — just as each additional light helps to dispel the darkness in a dimly lit hall.

~

A difference, in evolutionary standpoint, in spiritual development, in brain capacity, in physical strength, in health, in ability along definite lines — and even in possessions — will probably *always* exist.

But in the Coming Humanity, in a loving mutual understanding, no one will cause another's suffering: the greatest joy of everyone will be to use all that they are and have for the giving of joy to others. There will not be the misery of poverty — nor the curse of selfishly used wealth.

Your money values do not count with Me: *heart* values are the only things worthy of My consideration. With all your millions — with all the world's treasures — you cannot bribe Me to come. But where a pure heart is unfolding Self — though in its humbleness and lack of brilliance unnoticed by most of you — there am I attracted. *There* is the New Humankind coming into expression. *There* dawns the wider consciousness which will bring a perfect solution to all problems, of all mysteries.

The only mystery you need to solve is the realization of the Oneness of all life. Love *will* solve it — and therewith all your problems.

6
PURITY OF EMOTIONS

WHAT A WHIRLING and twirling in the super-
ethereal substance of your body and in your
atmosphere! Invisible to you, perhaps? But there,
nevertheless — as a result of your excitability, your
uncontrolled emotions, your restlessness.

Learn to *see*. Then watch the turbulent motions
of the fine matter on which emotions are impressed.
Watch the disturbances set up in the earthly atmosphere by the hurry and the struggle and nervosity
of modern life. Watch the superphysical conditions
of a city, of noisy traffic, of a celebrating crowd. Then,
too, of your own home. And of yourself!

But *you* are not emotional, are you? You are won-
derfully balanced. You can read in the daily papers,
without being in the least stirred, about battles rag-
ing where thousands are killed and maimed . . . but
none *you* know are there; about the destruction of
factories in which *you* have no shares; about cata-
clysms and calamities all far away from home; about
murders, holdups, etc. not in *your* neighborhood.

But — on the next page is a paragraph . . . look
again. Can that be right? A slump in your best stocks?
Your candidate exposed? A rumor about some scan-
dal in your family? Or your name honorably men-
tioned . . . so terribly misspelled that nobody will
know it is you? But that is more than anyone can
stand! *Now* watch the atmosphere!

What an agitation when your dinner is somewhat late, the soup is over-seasoned, and the coffee is served cold! You try to keep your poise, but from a gloomy face, you emanate muddy torrents which darken the whole house.

What horrid streaks in your aura, splashes of miry hues when you "enjoy" low emotional music or a passionate opera — which you like to call "art"! Or when reading obscene stories or exchanging vulgar jokes.

Such pastimes are to your emotions what salted pretzels are to the lining of the throat: artificially, they excite a thirst, a longing for satisfaction, entirely unnatural.

If only you could see what chaos you create with your applause, your yells, your screams, and unnecessary noises! They go fairly well with bullfights, with war dances, with feasts of savages, and orgies of uncouth brutes. At the present time, they *should* not — in the Coming Humankind, they *cannot* find a place!

Why permit them in your children, and encourage them in colleges and schools? Why do you go on with most of them? Because you *like* emotion? And do not care to know about Nature's finer forces? Because you are too filled with what you call "pleasure" to seek the nobler pleasures of the People I shall bring?

Emotion and excitement — could you live *without* these? Without your dinner parties, your theaters and shows; your tension about new quotations, your chance for special gains; your shopping, and selecting unneeded things at sales; your friendly (?) naggings and quarrels with your nearest relatives; your chats about the "latest" (quite confidentially, of course); your numberless appointments (all important, to be sure); and even your disappointments?

Days would seem dull and dreary if you had to miss these things. They are the stimulants that keep you going — the spices without which your life would be tedious indeed!

You have not yet transmuted your emotions. You are still negative. You are still being lived by outer influences — instead of positively *living* a life ruled by yourself, by the Self from within!

~

What then?

What can replace these things, which are now so coveted and without which existence seems insipid . . . to you who do not know?

Fear not.

Life will not be prosaic where I can manifest. I prompt no long-drawn faces; no yawns of irksomeness; no faintness; no depression; no attacks of melancholy. These are themselves the outcome of your emotionalism — unwholesome as it is. They will all be discarded when I come.

What is the song of birds to one who is totally deaf? What, a glorious sunset to the blind — or spiritually blinded? Can the uneducated grasp an artist's ecstasy? Could you *make* them understand while they still lack the needed faculties?

Neither, perhaps, will it be possible to make the enrapturing joy of My exalted Humanity comprehensible to *you* as long as you lack Love — and Purity.

All your emotional pleasures will be looked upon as playthings, with which young humanity — with its childlike consciousness — once amused itself.

Are you not longing for an expansion of your knowledge, for a capacity to be thrilled by now-unknown manifestations of life around and within you? Or would you, like some children, rather cling to your toys? Toys are quite useful — as long as the mind is weak. But if kept *too* long, they form obstacles to further growth. So does the unchecked play of your emotions: it hinders your unfoldment.

My Children will acquire that wider consciousness, which brings with it a comprehension, now undreamt of, of other worlds than yours; and a capability to approach the *cosmic* consciousness, at present vaguely sensed by only very few. This cosmic consciousness is as far above your own as yours is beyond that of the atoms of which your body is composed.

Expand your consciousness — by purifying your emotions. Help it to grow, to take in more and more — until, finally, it will be cosmic. As it unfolds, you will begin to realize the unity of all — and that brings love for all: *of* all, *for* all.

Then comes the happiness that never can be disturbed and which makes all work a joy.

The Coming People will live in the greatest joy: the joy of *giving* joy — the purest of pure emotions.

~

Emotion must not be killed — but it should be purified, transmuted, kept under strict control . . . under the control of Self.

Balance must be acquired — but *not* indifference. Balance is controlled emotion. Destroyed emotion is indifference.

Have you compassion? Do you weep with those who weep and suffer with those who suffer? And, in another hour, do you laugh with those who laugh and giggle with those who giggle? Then, even your compassion is but a play of your emotions.

Become compassionate! Learn to understand the cause of suffering. Look with the greatest love — with *understanding* love — upon the sufferers. Without yourself being swept by your emotions: will to help. Intuitively you will know *how*. Console. Relieve. Instruct. And bring good cheer.

Help all you can. Respond to every call of those who suffer. But never lose control of your emotions.

Thus will you show true compassion — and balance without indifference.

~

Be ever more sensitive — without being sentimental.

Not sensitive about things that bother *you*! Offenses or neglects, trespasses, ill luck, losses, and annoyances will not affect you anymore when you purify and master your emotions.

But sensitive to others so that you may understand and respond immediately to the needs of your surroundings. This selfless sensitiveness will naturally develop with the growth of *pure* emotions.

The New Humanity will be super-sensitive — yet not emotional.

The higher sensitiveness will open up the sensory organs to numberless new impressions: to natural phenomena, in the existence of which you now scarcely believe — because *you* are blind and deaf, your organs are still unfit to respond to a greater range of vibrations.

Things, now unseen, will become visible to My Children: colors of indescribable beauty and brilliance will loom before their eyes. The harmony of the spheres will become audible in music, free from the limitations of physical instruments. Perfumes, delicious and pure, will be found to fill the air. Things long heedlessly overlooked will fascinate humankind by their color, sound, and scent.

Immeasurable treasures will Nature reveal in limitless abundance to the Children of the New Humanity.

That is: to *you* — if you prepare for it, if you purify your emotions.

7
PURITY OF THOUGHTS

WHAT WOULD YOU DO? If you could see the thoughts of everyone around you — what would you do?

Be glad you do *not* see them! Those concerning you might seriously disturb your self-sufficient complacency. And an unsuspected knowledge of the thoughts of others about their business and their private affairs might lead you to selfishly abuse such secret information.

Yet: you *will* see them when you come into My Humanity! But by that time, you will have lost all touch with selfishness.

If every thought of yours could be seen by other people — what would you do?

Would you want them to be seen? Would you dare to have them seen? I fear you are often glad in your conviction that others *cannot* see.

But: all *will* see your thoughts in the New Humankind!

～

If your every thought — no matter on what subject, however definite or vague — could now be seen by Those Who (though invisible and perhaps unknown to you) are guiding and teaching you, helping your evolution, preparing you to become eligible candidates for My noble, peerless Humanity, what would you do?

They *do* see them!

And so do I.

It is upon the quality of your thoughts — more than upon anything else — that you are judged by Them. Essentially, upon your thoughts, your very growth depends. The amount of Love and Purity you put into your thoughts — *that* will decide whether you can pass into the Future Humanity.

Your every thought is watched — even the faintest impulse of a thought is noted. And every occurrence — even the slightest incident in your everyday life — is utilized as a test: to see what kind of thought it will arouse; for nothing and no-one should have the power to bring out undesirable thoughts in you.

The result is automatically registered, indelibly: each thought sets up vibrations in superphysical matter, impressing upon it an ever-lasting record, which is an open book to Me. Many a page is soiled, unworthy, and most often worthless. In vain, I look for definitely pure and worthy, loving and constructive thoughts which will help to bring humanity nearer to the day on which I can manifest in the magnificent New Generation of People!

How does *your* record stand?

What will you do to make it better? What are you adding from hour to hour?

What will you do?

~

You doubt My words?

That does not change the fact: that I *do* see all your thoughts. Even your most secret thoughts are not hidden from Me. Even merely passing ones are noticeable to Me. I see them even before you have put them through the process of shaping them in your brain!

For, in the spiritual realms — where I dwell — thoughts, *all* your thoughts, are palpable, tangible things.

Thoughts are things — *real* things — things that you have created!

~

In your little material world of deceptive appearances, you judge each other almost exclusively by the clothes you wear. And by a shrewd selection of your garments, you try to convince others that you are what you are *not*.

But to My eye, you wear quite another cloak! You are surrounded by the forms created by your thoughts. That is the garb you make for yourself, into which you weave every thread, draw every design, frame every pattern. That is the apparel that shows what you really *are*.

And what an object it presents of most of you!

A shapeless, slovenly bundle of dirty rags, of unattractive, muddy colors, patched and pinned together without any apparent plan, with far too many "I's" and grasping hooks — and full of holes and gaps, showing the emptiness of your existence, your lack of thought.

Such is the attire in which you show yourself to Me — and to all those who *can* see.

In the New Humankind, all will see. But none will enter it who have not changed their robe — making it presentable and pleasing to the clear-seeing eye. None but those who have purified their thoughts, and ensouled them with love, will be admitted into My People of the Future.

⁓

Through your thoughts, you create your own future: what you think you will *be*!

By concentrated thought, you create a form of what you wish to become. After this pattern, if you make it strong enough, you — your conditions and your body — will be shaped.

This is dangerous knowledge. For you want things selfishly. Your desire is to be rich or famous: to *shine*, to stand out above your fellows in power, wealth, learning, or artistic ability. And you want even spirituality . . . only to be more than others.

Therefore, *practical* knowledge of the creative power of thought is being withheld from you. You would utilize it for selfish purposes. And so, you would stunt your evolution — and that of humanity, of which each one of you is an integral part. You would intensify the hampering influence of the "self" — and thus prevent the coming-into-expression of the Self.

Once you are selfless — once you are less a slave to your paltry little "self" — you will learn how to create instantaneously and visibly by thought. This, the Children of My People, will have learned to do. Their knowledge will be applied only for others' sake — never for their own.

All of them will be artists — in that *new* art: the making of exquisite thoughts, which everyone else, with the sense of clearer sight, will be able to enjoy.

More beautiful than the greatest treasures of art, now kept in your museums and stored away in private galleries, will be their works — produced by all, for all.

⌒

Thought is the ultimate creative power.

Sound creates in physical matter, but wise, thoughtful beings first consciously *think* — they first consciously create by thought, in subtler matter, that which will serve as a model for their physical creations.

The Great Power who created the Universe created it *by thought* — before, by His spoken Word, He brought it down into physical manifestation. If you consider yourself to be made in His image — do as He did: and think . . . before you speak.

First, in the realm of thought are made the archetypes for all things physical in the Macrocosm. So do you, by your thoughts, create the patterns for all that will occur in your future microcosm.

⌒

Strong, definite, oft-repeated thoughts build living entities — even though you do not see them. If you nourish them and give them regular attention, they will do obediently what you charge them to do. Whatever quality — of hate or love, of healing or destruction — *you* put into them will be their motive power, their actual life force.

Strong thoughts are rare — and fortunately so: if there were many, the evil, grasping, selfish ones would far outnumber the unselfish.

Such is present humanity. But in the New, rid of all selfishness, all will know how to build beneficent, entrancing forms.

You think no vitally harmful, no violently hateful, not even essentially self-seeking thoughts, do you? Just a perpetual succession of the smallest, faintest thoughts of personal criticisms, of personal dislikes, of trivial personal wishes — are these your average thoughts? They may *seem* harmless — but they do not build a world in which I can manifest!

After all, they are more harmful than you now realize.

These countless millions of diminutive vague thoughts, continually sent out by most of you, are — by the Law that like attracts like — drawn to each other. They strengthen one another, forming what might be called: great reservoirs of force.

These — good or bad — when filled to overflowing, empty themselves upon humanity. Rarely is one containing love and kindness filled to the point where it is ready for distribution. But frequently, contents of a less enjoyable nature are poured out. Then comes catastrophe or epidemic, pestilence, or war. All are of humanity's own making: resulting from their thoughts. Each person receives what they have put in — by the accumulation of their own thoughtless thinking, of their own unchecked thoughts.

Not till you purify your thoughts will these horrors cease.

Not till you leave all harmful elements, *all* selfish proclivities out of your thoughts, will suffering and sorrow be no more attracted by you.

Not till, determinedly, you direct the pure power of your thoughts toward helping others can I manifest in you.

Not till there is Purity in your every deed, in your every word, and in your every thought will — where you are — the Coming Humanity be born.

❀

EPILOGUE

*Exalted and exultant beyond
the most fanciful visions of today's
idealists will be My Radiant Humanity —
which will soon be established.*

THE PRESENT HUMANITY AND THE NEW

I AM NO DREAMER, visualizing things as they might be! I *know* what is to be!

Behind some dreamers of utopias, I stood, inspiring them, guiding their thoughts — that through their works, the world might see the future and exert its efforts to approach the day when I shall come to establish the New Humankind.

My hints they worked out according to *their* viewpoint — and used them to support that single fraction of the Truth which they had recognized.

But now I speak Myself, with definite knowledge of what is planned to be — of what already *is* in the Universal Mind, existing even now in the highest realms of thought, which to My vision, are more real than trees and stones to yours.

I am not merely "dreaming" when I speak of the Coming Humanity — for I am the Spirit of that Humankind!

But on you, the people of today, on you, it will depend *when* it will be established — when, with its joy and peace, its splendor, its unequaled happiness, it will come down into physical expression.

～

I, Spirit of the Unborn, have indicated — in My Plea for Purity — some of the changes essentially needed in preparing the world, and yourselves, for the New Humanity.

Now I shall synthesize the differences between the present people and My People of tomorrow.

The keynote of the present humanity is to *have*; that of the New: to *be*.

You try to obtain, be it for the benefit of yourself or for others, whatever outer things may seem desirable. But no matter what you possess — it *can* be lost again and *will* be lost sooner or later.

Try to become — help others to become, to build into themselves eternal qualities: the only things that *never* can be lost. Then will you help the coming of the New Humankind.

The present humanity seeks to *grasp*; the New will live to *give*.

Large incomes, high positions, accumulation of private property, personal satisfaction — that is what all the world is seeking these days. "Giving" is looked upon as "sacrifice," as "renunciation" — and whenever it is practiced, it is usually prompted by the hope of some return.

In My Humankind, "giving" will be the general expression of the people's selflessness; it will be their keenest joy.

The watchword of the present humanity is *competition*; that of the New will be *cooperation*.

Beginning in your schools, the training is: to outrival the other student, in learning, in sport. And all through life, this system is kept up: put others into the shade, *compete*.

Life-poisoning competition has done its share in the plan of evolution: in helping to develop the concrete mind. But this is not the highest that humanity can gain!

With the New People comes *transmuted* competition: there, all will vie in giving others what they would most desire for themselves. Each, knowing that they share the One Life with their kin, will do their utmost for the common good. Without reserve, all will wholeheartedly cooperate.

The present humanity is *destructive*; the New will be *constructive*.

Watch children: how, almost without exception — they enjoy destroying things. Adults encourage them and eagerly assist in the destruction of *living things*. The propensity is checked — by rules of propriety and, mainly, of police.

By their injurious emanations, humankind has estranged the many ethereal, now invisible beings who exist and evolve alongside them. They have filled them with distrust and disgust. The New People will be harmless and helpful to all that co-exists — thereby regaining the kind assistance of the Nature-spirits, who will beautify the world, accomplishing their joyous task before the purified eye of humanity.

The elements themselves will cooperate with them and will no longer destroy — by cyclones, earthquakes, floods, or fire, by extremes of heat and cold — what human beings have wrought. All these catastrophes are caused by *humanity itself*: resulting from their destructive attitude toward Nature, as well as from their thoughts.

In the New Humankind, new inventions will utilize enormous powers which will be revealed in Nature — and in themselves; and these will be available for great constructive work. They are still kept unknown because, under the control of a *destructive* humanity, they would be dangerous.

Sex inequality is a mighty factor in present humanity; in the New, *sex equality* will prevail.

The mystification of the process of reproduction; the secrecy attached to natural forms; unwarranted prudishness and pseudo-ignorance; the over-accentuation of sex differences in dress, in education, in mannerism — all these promote furtive thoughts and stealthy whisperings concerning sexology fomenting sensuality, refined as it may be.

In My luminous Humankind, sex will be recognized as a minor incident. There will be little difference in dress, in expression — even in character: both sexes will more equally manifest the highest that is now in each.

Knowledge, scientific knowledge, is the glory of the present humanity; but in the New, *Wisdom* will be supreme.

Science, however admirable, deals with the *outer*, with the phenomenal side. It is a slow, slow process toward the heart of things! Not from the outside in — but from the inside out, is wisdom's way.

Within is the One Life. Seek to know *that*! Turn your attention within yourself: you can find it there. That same Life manifests in others and is the motive power in all Nature's phenomena. Once you attain a realization of it — which can be done by utmost Purity — you know the *cause*, the how and why of everything: perfected wisdom will include all knowledge.

The present humanity is led by *intellect*; the Coming will be led by *intuition*.

Intellectuality is the ability to conceive intelligently the actualities in the world around you — as far as they can be observed by your defective and imperfect instruments and organs of perception. It depends entirely upon impressions of the brain from the outside.

Whereas intuition is tuition *from within*: it brings unlimited, true knowledge of the Self. When you completely open yourself to it, you will know all there is to know in the entire Universe. For, in your Self, you can share the consciousness of all and of *the all* — in your Self, you are One *with all*.

The present humanity has *religions*; the New will have *religion*.

Religions are the garments in which the Divine has sheathed Itself in order to remain perceptible to the spiritually blinded eyes of human souls. And as the soul-eyes differed — so has Divinity shown Itself in different cloaks.

But true religion enables human beings to see *through* every garment, perceiving the Divine in its Purity within the Same in *all* — manifesting not alone in Its garments of religions but in everything and everywhere.

In the New Humankind, the true meaning of religion: the reunion of people with God, will be fully understood — and this reunion will be accomplished by each one of My Children individually and directly, without the need for doctrines, dogmas, rites, or creeds.

The present humanity is surrounded by *ugliness*; in *beauty* will the New one be enveloped.

Your standard of beauty is guided by cost and rarity: most of the articles you value for their "beauty," you would not deign to look upon if they were cheap if they could be possessed by everyone. Your preference for the beautiful is, as a rule, a seeking of personal gratification — and grossly selfish.

In the New Humankind, art and beauty will be a *result* of inner purity — instead of having for their aim, as they now do, the demonstration of outer superiority.

It is the beauty of the *senses* which is sought by the present humanity, but in the New, the beauty of the *spirit* will be predominant. Soul beauty will find expression in feature and in form, in gracefully rhythmic motions, in pleasing, melodious voices, and in kind, loving acts. The beauty attained within will cause all outer objects to be beautiful.

Not by contemptuously shunning, not by repugnantly repelling from your presence all that is still ugly, can the beauty of My Humankind be gained: only by purifying, only by beautifying one's inner nature, can it be acquired.

When that is achieved, the ugly *can* no longer exist. Then, Nature itself will be magnificent as it has never been — because humankind will no longer interfere with the work of its agents. It will open up its hidden gamers and spread its treasures of unexampled beauty over the Earth. And the radiance of good cheer and of supreme enjoyment will be on every face: on yours, when you will be reborn into My resplendent Humankind — or, on yours *now* if you prepare yourself to be selected as one of those who will lay its foundation.

The present humanity stoops under a load of *suffering*; the New, with a lifted head, will reflect the light from Heaven, which is the purest *joy*.

Stop *causing* your own misery by self-centeredness, by shutting off your "self" from the joy-giving luminosity of the Self!

More radiant than the sun's beams is the Self. Let it shine within you and enlighten you — filling with its great and imperturbable joy all the dark chambers in your being. It will do that — if you cleanse the windows and do not keep the shades and shutters of your selfish separateness closed. It *will* — if you concentrate your efforts and thoroughly purify yourself.

This is why I plead with you: that even now, your suffering may be lightened and that you may begin to know the all-surpassing joy in which the New People will live.

The present humanity is marked by *separateness*; the New will be distinguished by *unity*.

Each one now prides themselves on what they have that others do not have — and attention is given exclusively to *differences* in possessions, in race, in dress, ability, political convictions, and religious beliefs.

My People seek that which *unites*. And as each one will realize that they themselves, that their own inner Self, their Life, *is* God — and that all else that lives are themselves, because it is, in essence, the same Self, the same Life, the same God — none can any longer feel interests separate from those of others.

Try to realize now: that you really *are* the others!

The present humanity is *attached*; the New will be *detached*.

Attached to physical forms and formalities, to outer appearances, is present humanity. Even in its friendships, in its love, it clings to the matter side.

The New People will know the spirit side of all manifestation: it will deal with the eternal. Therefore, it will be detached, freed from the deceptive ties of temporary objects, freed from the fear of losing whatever it may have — and hence free from *all* fear.

The present humanity is *personal*; the New will be *impersonal*.

Your personality is considered all-important: its wants, its wishes, its opinions, its interests, its well-being — these fill your life, your thoughts.

As yet, it seems almost useless to speak to you of your Impersonality — of the One Self *within* yourself, which links you up with all!

My People will be free from the despotism of the selfish, personal "self" — acknowledging alone the absolute supremacy of the selfless and *impersonal* great Self.

Limitation holds the present humanity in bounds; Mine, throwing off all shackles, will attain *liberation*.

Imprisoned, vastly limited are you in your self-expression — even if you know it not! Your selfishness restrains you; your materialistic intellect confines you; your separative principles entomb the real "You."

By subjugation of your "self," unfetter your true Self! Then, you will triumph over every limitation — and, as a member of My mighty Humankind, reach liberation from all ignorance, all suffering, all woe.

Break away from the detention of the *declining* self in the *plethora* of "selves" — and consciously share the Oneness of the evolved liberated Self!

These few points of contrast indicate the trend of My New Humanity — and what it will mean to you if you can enter it.

Then you will realize that all the world *is you*.

Then, you will be at one with every living creature, with everything that *is*: with sky and trees and ocean, with elements, with insects, birds, and beasts, with fellow beings, with gods — and yes: with God.

Then, you will know that you are immortal — that you *have always been* and will never cease to be.

Then, you will consciously feel the power of God pass through you to others — and pour out the Divine Life in all its greatness and its glory over others.

Then, you will be aware that there is a never-ending unfoldment of Divinity in you, *in all*, that a greater and ever greater expansion — an unlimited succession of incomparable and wonderful attainments — lies before you.

Then, you will find yourself receptive to sensations such as a little human soul can scarcely comprehend — and in comparison with which, all that is now considered "happiness" sink into nothingness.

This is the promise for My triumphant Humankind!

UNIVERSAL LOVE

L OVE IS THE UNITING POWER of the Great Cosmic Magnet.

Whatever *is*, is a particle of that Magnet: apart from It — yet always held bound to It by this inherent faculty of Love.

Be it only manifest in the form of cohesion, of gravity, of chemical affinity — it is the same uniting force of Love. Be it greed, or longing, or personal attraction — it is the working of the same principle: a lean toward unity with something else.

It is true: many an atom seems sadly demagnetized because — by cold mentality — it has gone far away from the Great Magnet; because it has shrunk into the form of a closed circle, keeping the current flowing *within itself*, wholly self-centered, loving only the own "self."

But every fragment gradually unfolds its inborn quality . . . into pure, self-forgetting, personal love. As it evolves its inner power, it is lifted up in the direction of its Source, so it will reach the point where the direct current of the Great Magnet is near enough to fill it with Its own original potency: of Universal Love.

Pure personal love is the ultimate accomplishment of *your* generation.

When you enter into the stream of Universal Love, you enter into My Generation.

~

All personal love is limited and exclusive — hence, an imperfect demonstration of Divine Love. But . . . do not underestimate the value it has for you; do not be misled by the fallacious thought that you can rise above it by ignoring its exalting influence.

Only by the perfecting of the highest personal love can you be lifted up to where the constant Current of Universal Love can touch — and flow through — you.

Great personal love is gradually developed by memories of happiness shared in the past with beloved ones, strengthened through many lives, growing from selfish passion into unselfish, pure — be it still personal — love.

While it evolves, one learns to share lovingly the *sorrows* of the beloved. Out of this, compassion grows — by which the power is acquired to feel with, and *in* others, more and more.

Both — the compassion and the personal love — must by your efforts be intensified, augmented to the highest attainable degree, in order to prepare you for the influx of the Universal Love and, thereby, for My Humankind.

~

Perfect, unlimited, and all-inclusive is Universal Love. When it becomes manifest in you, all are as near to you as the dearest you love now. And it expands until, without distinction, you love all — until you have fully realized that *all* are only One, that all *are* "You."

Universal Love is *not* the personal love, parceled out in negligible minims to every creature — *not* personal love, diluted into indifferent kindness for all, without kinship for any.

It is a new outpouring of Divinity in you, the acquisition of a wider consciousness, at the point where you can step out of the present humanity into My spiritualized Kind — where you can break the shell that limits full-grown humanity, in order to enter into the infancy of super-humanity.

PERFECT PURITY

For Purity — for *perfect* Purity — have I, the Spirit of the Unborn, been pleading with you, in order that My People of purified Humanity may come into manifested existence.

Soon I shall select a few of you to establish it in a secluded place — where conditions will be ideally suitable. Some I *have* found who are ready; more I *expect* to find in the near future. But not until a sufficient number is prepared can My Humankind be founded definitely, as a segregated unit.

I have therefore come to lay before you all those qualities that will be indispensable if you wish to join the early settlement of the New Humanity.

Purity and Love are the fundamental needs — not only for admission into My Humankind; for in the course of time, no one can progress very far without Love and Purity!

The purity that I require is one not only of deeds but of every word and thought, and not only of your thoughts but of your very *being*, of your whole nature! So pure you must be that not any influence from the outside can awaken an undesirable response in you.

This may seem almost impossible for anyone of you to attain perfectly. But if you strive — and *refuse* to be ruled, even for a single moment, by other principles than those of Purity and of Love — then you will see improvement from day to day, and the tendency to yield to less worthy influences will rapidly lose its hold upon you. Thus will you become a candidate for My Humanity.

Has it no attraction for you? Does it appear to you as if devoid of interest, monotonous, nonsensical, absurd? Only the narrow-minded can thus misjudge what, in the course of evolution — in the growth of consciousness, of liberty, of *joy* — still awaits them.

All will attain sometime. The choice I bring is this: will you grow willingly, helping the cosmic Law and hastening evolution — or blindly struggle on, unknowingly, even *unwillingly*, and remaining so much longer in the misery of your half-evolved stage?

~

I, the Spirit of the Unborn, have come to call for aspirants for the Coming Humankind!

I am its Spirit — and I am even *more*. I am the Spirit — of the New Humanity — and of *all beings*. I am — the Spirit!

But I have spoken only in this one aspect: as Spirit of the Unborn — because for their, as well as for your sake, the New People must soon be born.

I have not called in vain!

I have not called without arousing some of you to the significance of what I have stated: that a New Humankind is about to be established.

What I want *everyone* to know — what I have wanted you to know and understand all through this message is this.

The Unborn of New Ideal People is ready for your world when you are ready for them.

They will come when you prepare their way.

They are waiting for purer bodies, purer surroundings, purer parents, and purer Love.

They will incarnate as soon as you are pure; and *you yourself* can enter My New Humankind — when you steadily strive for perfect Purity.

I AM WAITING!

THANK YOU FOR READING!

I F YOU ENJOYED THIS BOOK, please consider leaving a review, even if it is only a line or two. It would make all the difference and would be very much appreciated.

Sign up for our newsletter to be the first to know when new books are published:

radiantbooks.co/bonus

Printed in Great Britain
by Amazon

28557653R00058